Thomas J. Taylor

Ethereum Concise

Ethereum Concise

Ethereum for Beginners: The Basics on History, Present and Future, Ethereum and Ethereum Classic, Ether, Ethereum Tokens, DApps, Smart Contracts and Ethereum Wallets

Thomas J. Taylor

Table of contents

Foreword

I am convinced that Ethereum is here to stay.

At the time of writing, there are over 8,540 cryptocurrencies[1] (although "currency" is a big and actually wrong word here). Most of them will go under again due to their limited usability, or simply because they are fake.

Ethereum will exist.

Ethereum is more than a coin, in fact it is not even primarily a coin, it is an infrastructure, a system based on the blockchain that provides a platform for multiple uses. The payment option within this system is the Ether.

With the transition to proof-of-stake clients, it will become even more future-proof. The transformation will be completed in 2022 as Ethereum 2.0.

---

[1] https://coinmarketcap.com

Chapter 1:
The history of Ethereum

The concept of Ethereum was first described in a whitepaper.[2] The whitepaper (a document that describes the goals of a project and also attempts to quantify the indicative timeframe and, essentially, the core) described the mechanisms of the Ethereum platform for creating decentralized applications based on smart contracts. We could see the paper for the first time in 2013.

Right from the start, the new idea of creating a platform to use blockchain technology not only for decentralized money (as is the case with Bitcoin, for example) was taken up by a large number of startups and companies.

The idea to create this platform came from a Canadian programmer with Russian roots, Vitalik Buterin. Not everyone knows that Vitalik himself was and is also a big supporter of Bitcoin.

He founded and edited Bitcoin Magazine, the first blog dedicated to all information about Bitcoins from a technical and developmental perspective.

---

[2] https://ethereum.org/en/whitepaper/

In 2013, Bitcoin Magazine, co-founded and edited by Vitalik, published an article describing the concept of the Ethereum platform.

In the initial phase, the main idea was to create a platform for the development of a decentralized application ("DApp")[3] and integrate it with the Bitcoin network.

However, this proposal was rejected by the Bitcoin community.

The creation and development of a dedicated blockchain for the use of smart contracts later became the main goal of the project.

According to Vitalik, the name "Ethereum" was taken from Wikipedia and means "medium that permeates the universe and allows light to travel."

The announcement of a new project was published on January 23, 2014 in the article "Ethereum: now going public", which provided a detailed description of the platform, smart contract, cryptocurrency and decentralized autonomous organization ("DAO").

---

[3] An application where elementary states and values are stored not only on one server or computer but on many different machines, a network of machines.

In June 2014, the Ethereum Foundation, a non-profit foundation, was established to support the creation and development of this platform.

The project's ICO[4] took place from July 20 to September 2, 2014. During this time, the developers were able to collect about thirty-one thousand Bitcoins, which at that time was equivalent to about eighteen million dollars.

In this regard, we recall that during the pre-sale phase, you could still get two thousand Ethereum for one Bitcoin (today it's still around 14 Ethereum).

Moreover, for better understanding, we can say that today we would have to spend over $9 million to buy two thousand Ethereum.

The platform has been tested since early February 2014, when the proof of concept Ethereum was launched.

The first public test network was launched in 2015 and was named Olympic.

At this point, users were intentionally trying to clog the network with transactions by creating nodes and trying to disrupt the network itself, and among other

---

4 Initial Coin Offering

things, they received some sort of premium for all of this, paid in Ethereum by the foundation itself.

Olympic was the last phase in the development of Ethereum before the launch of the basic network implementation called Frontier.

The main development phase of Ethereum was divided into several parts so that the development process was smooth and consistent.

July 30, 2015 has always been considered the actual launch day of the network, because that was the day the first version of the network, namely the Frontier network, was launched.

An important feature of this version was that the developers did not guarantee the security and reliability of the platform.

Frontier was aimed in particular at developers and experienced technology users, i.e. not newcomers. Actually, these experienced users should form an active ecosystem.

With this version, users could initiate transactions, extract, create and test smart contracts and DApps.

Another important feature of this version was the so-called "canary contracts", i.e. contracts that alternated between the values one and zero.

Each order was controlled by members of the development team.

In fact, the developers were able to override the actions of users on the network, so it was by no means possible to speak of a decentralized concept.

But the next step to increase the popularity of the platform was the Ethereum-based ICO.

The ICO concept was introduced in 2013 during a fundraiser for the MasterCoin project, which was later named OmniLayer, i.e. a digital currency and communication protocol based on Bitcoin's blockchain, providing a secure transaction solution for Bitcoin 2.0.

Ethereum thus became a platform that would lay the groundwork for smart contracts with the ability to create cryptocurrency tokens.

It enabled the creation of new tokens on its blockchain using the ERCERC-20 protocol.

Ethereum's first ICO took place on August 17, 2015, and formed the basis for the decentralized prediction market project Augur (decentralized and open-source platform for market predictions built on Ethereum).

During the ICO, REP tokens raised over five million dollars.

This event triggered the ICO boom on the Ethereum platform and a FOMO[5] that led to the crypto world opening up to the average user, but also saw many scammers at work.

In 2016, Homestead, the first stable version of the protocol, was released.

In this version of the network, the "canary contracts" were disabled and changes were made to the EIP (Ethereum Improvement Proposal), which should in some way improve protection against spam attacks and network incompatibility of future changes to the protocol.

The EIPs were proposed to improve the use of Ethereum outside the network.

All subsequent updates to Homestead have been hard forks[6] with the sole purpose of improving the platform.

One of the possibilities of blockchain is also the creation of previously mentioned decentralized auto-

---

[5] A "Fear of missing out" (acronym FOMO) is a form of social anxiety/fear/concern.

[6] Modification of a network in such a way that backward compatibility is no longer possible. Splitting the blockchain into an old and new version.

nomous organizations (DAOs), i.e. a type of organization based on a smart contract that governs how an organization makes decisions.

DAO tokens give voting rights and control to their holders.

The Ethereum development team, along with a group from the startup Slock.it, has developed "The DAO," a decentralized organization built on the Ethereum blockchain.

For the first time, an organization has been created where members can monitor their invested funds in real time.

The management process has been handled by automated systems, creating nothing more than a digital enterprise managed by the community itself.

After the crowdsale of "The DAO" on April 30, 2016, about one hundred and fifty million dollars were raised by twenty thousand investors.

However, on June 17, the project was attacked and around three and a half million Ethereum were stolen.

The attackers used a vulnerability called "recursive" that many community members had reported a week before the attack, but the Slock.it team did not take the warnings seriously, which cost the project fifty million dollars and led to the complete collapse of "The DAO".

It also allowed the smart contract user to withdraw twice as much Ether as they had invested and transfer the money to Child DAO.

This is due to a typo in the code. The stolen funds could not be withdrawn because there was a twenty-seven day window of opportunity when the Child DAO was created. The developers took this time to find solutions to the problem, but the only thing the developers could do to recover the stolen funds was to opt for a hard fork.

The larger pool miners voted on whether they were willing to implement the hard fork.

Most miners agreed, and so it was decided to return the invested Ethereum to the users.

All DAO tokens were frozen and sent to a new address so that participants could withdraw their invested funds.

There was some disagreement in the community over the decision of most to do a hard fork.

For this reason, it was decided to restore the system to its state before the creation of "The DAO", thus invalidating the stolen Ethereum.

This was a controversial decision, as part of the group that disagreed with the decision stated that this would violate the principle of decentralization, as the blockchain should and must be immutable and smart contracts must remain self-sufficient.

Thus, the crypto community ended up with two independent blockchains: Ethereum, which returned funds to investors and now ranks second in market capitalization among all cryptocurrencies, and Ethereum Classic, which retained the original blockchain.

However, we must point out that the Ethereum Classic community is working today to improve interoperability between the two blockchains and has its own troubled development history.

After the hack of the DAO project, the price of Ethereum fell by almost half and hovered around eleven dollars.

The essential at a glance

- ⇨ The concept of Ethereum was first described in 2013.
- ⇨ "Inventor" of Ethereum is Vitalik Buterin.
- ⇨ Ethereum Classic is a fork of Ethereum, which is no longer as significant as Ethereum.

Chapter 2: What is Ethereum?

As mentioned, Ethereum is the second largest force in the cryptocurrency sector in terms of market capitalization, after Bitcoin.

In the golden year of virtual currencies, Ethereum was often associated with the notion of the new Bitcoin.

In reality, these are two different projects.

Ethereum is a decentralized virtual computer whose goal is to develop and manage smart contracts.

Virtual because it is a computer on the network made up of all the other computers on the Ethereum network. Decentralized because no one can attack, censor, or control it.

From what has been said, we can immediately understand that Ethereum is much more than a cryptocurrency as understood by those who are new to this field. And besides, the virtual currency is technically called Ether (abbreviation ETH, symbol: Ξ).

In defining Ethereum, it is necessary to mention both Smart Contracts and Ether, two concepts that deserve a separate discussion.

To further clarify the differences, it is also important to point out what the real difference is between Ethereum and Bitcoin.

Ether is Ethereum's cryptocurrency, which is purchased by network participants to pay for the use of computing power, without which smart contracts could not exist.

In simpler terms, we can define Ether as the gasoline that powers a machine called Ethereum.

So if we equate the word cryptocurrency with Ethereum, we would be making a mistake.

The digital currency is Ether, which can also be seen as a kind of incentive for user-developers to create higher quality applications.

In fact, for Ethereum, Ether is the counterpart of Bitcoin and the network's internal payment system.

Let's take a look at Ethereum's year-over-year performance together, with market capitalization (in US dollars) in the historical report:

- January 1, 2016: 72 million

- January 1, 2017: 715 million

- January 1, 2018: 74.7 billion

- January 1, 2019: 14.6 billion

- January 1, 2020: 13.9 billion

- January 1, 2021: 88.4 billion

The last all-time high Ethereum reached was on November 10, 2021, at $4,859.50. In the fourth quarter of 2021, the market capitalization of Ethereum was partially around billion540 US dollars.

The capitalization of the cryptocurrency Ether has grown disproportionately in 2021.

Ethereum is thus the starting point for a new era on the Internet:

- It integrates currency and payments.
- Users can manage their own data, and the applications do not spy or steal data.
- Everyone has access to an open financial system.
- It is based on a neutral and open infrastructure and is not controlled by companies or individuals.

From this it can be deduced,

- That Ethereum is safe because no one can control it or manipulate it for their own benefit,
- that it is reliable because there is no single guarantor, but the network is formed by many users who confirm the operations performed,
- That it is transparent because all operations are public and can be reviewed by anyone and,
- that it is everywhere, because it is everywhere there is an Internet network.

In other words, we could think of Ethereum as a computer that works on many devices around the world simultaneously and therefore cannot have a single owner.

While it allows us to transfer digital money, it also allows us to implement code and interact with applications created by other users.

So the idea behind Ethereum is that developers can create and implement code that runs over a distributed network, rather than existing on a centralized server. This means that, in theory, these applications cannot be blocked or censored.

The applications are added to the Ethereum platform, i.e. the blockchain, and can be programmed in such a way that the code cannot be changed.

Also, the database is visible to all, so users can review the code before working with it.

This means that anyone and everyone anywhere can launch applications that cannot be disabled. Even more interesting is that these applications can set conditions for how value is transferred.

In most cases, the programs that make up smart contract applications can be configured to operate without human intervention.

The essential at a glance

- ⇨ Ethereum is an open platform based on the blockchain.
- ⇨ Ether (abbreviation ETH, symbol: Ξ) is the currency of Ethereum.
- ⇨ Ethereum enables the use of smart contracts (smart contracts) and DApps (decentralized applications).

Chapter 3:
Ethereum and Bitcoin

As mentioned in previous chapters, Ethereum has a computing platform and programming language that developers can use to create smart contracts and decentralized applications called DApps.

Developers can leverage the computing power of a global, decentralized network of computers on the Ethereum platform to create these smart contracts and DApps.

Bitcoin also has a global, decentralized computer network, although its computing power is primarily used to process transactions.

Bitcoin has neither a programming language nor a computing platform like Ethereum, but both have their own blockchains to record data.

While Bitcoin adds a new block to the Bitcoin blockchain about every ten minutes, Ethereum adds a new block to the Ethereum blockchain about every thirty seconds.

As for the currency, you have to consider the additional features Ethereum has over Bitcoin, and at first glance, you might think Ethereum is superior and could replace Bitcoin as the dominant cryptocurrency.

However, Ethereum is not intended as a replacement for Bitcoin. The two currencies were developed for different reasons and are in no way in competition with each other.

Bitcoin was the first cryptocurrency and the first blockchain network.

The currency in the Bitcoin network, also called Bitcoin, was created for financial transactions.

Moreover, Bitcoin is a global currency that exists outside the control of governments and financial institutions.

The Ethereum network currency, called "Ether," was developed to be used as a payment method for computing power on the Ethereum platform.

When a developer wants to run an application on the Ethereum platform, he buys the computing power in Ether.

Ether is also outside the control of governments and financial institutions, although Ether is intended to be a local currency for the Ethereum platform.

The number of Bitcoins is set at twenty-one million Bitcoins to avoid devaluing the price of Bitcoin by offering too much.

With Ethereum, on the other hand, there is no limit to the number of Ethers that can be created, and this means that the Ether price could fall if supply increases.

There are a variety of websites and stores around the world that accept Bitcoin as a form of payment.

As Bitcoin grows in popularity, it will become more widely accepted as a payment method alongside credit cards, PayPal, and cash.

You can pay for goods and services with Bitcoins, both online and in stores.

By the end of 2021, Bitcoin's market capitalization will be around USD 1000 billion, while Ether's will be around half of that.

Ethereum is not intended to be used as a payment method in stores and on websites.

As its popularity grows, Ethereum will become increasingly accepted as a platform for developing applications in competing programming languages, operating systems, and computer servers.

Developers and companies buy Ether to use as payment for computing power to be used on the Ethereum network.

The essential at a glance

- ⇨ Bitcoin is the largest (market capitalization at the end of 2021: about 1000 billion USD) cryptocurrency
- ⇨ Ether is the second largest (market capitalization at the end of 2021: around USD 500 billion) cryptocurrency
- ⇨ Bitcoin is primarily for payment settlements
- ⇨ Ethereum is a platform, used for applications, Ether is the associated currency

Chapter 4:
Ethereum Classic

I would also like to provide you with a comprehensive explanation of the difference between Ethereum and Ethereum Classic:

Compared to Bitcoin and Ethereum, which were created for different purposes, the same cannot be said of Ethereum and Ethereum Classic, as they are based on the same code and are similar to each other.

However, there are important differences.

We have already talked about the disagreements in the Ethereum community that led to the creation of the two Ethereum blockchains.

Originally, there was only one platform and one Ethereum currency, but due to a bug in the code of a smart contract known as "The DAO," the community split into two separate blockchains and currencies.

"The DAO" was one of the largest projects ever crowdfunded and had more than one hundred and fifty million dollars in Ether, about fifteen percent of total Ether reserves.

The bug in the smart contract code was not a vulnerability or an issue with Ethereum, because as we said, there were no issues with the Ethereum platform.

The smart contract had a flaw that was exploited and resulted in the theft of fifty million dollars in Ether. This flaw essentially consisted of a contract with a poorly written clause that allowed one party to exploit the contract.

If this were the case with a contract, one would turn to a court and to lawyers who would discuss the real reason for the clause, but with a smart contract there is nothing of the sort.

The code of the contract is the law.

The code was correct, but poorly worded.

The hackers managed to steal fifty million dollars in Ether through the poorly written contract. They didn't hack the system, they just found a piece of code that allows the transfer of funds between them under the smart contract.

The Ethereum community voted to cancel the contract as this was not the intention of the code.

Part of the community argued that it was not a hack and that the smart contract was therefore valid.

By canceling the deals, the community would act as judge and tribunal, deciding which contracts and deals are valid.

By cancelling the transactions, it would act as a third party intermediary and decide to modify the contracts concluded on the platform.

This went against the original intentions of the Ethereum platform, which was to be decentralized and free from the rules of any government, company, or third party.

If the terms of a smart contract are valid, it should not be cancelled; the code of the smart contract should be the law.

Due to the amount of money stolen, the community voted to cancel the transactions and the money was returned.

This means that one of the parties to a contract acted as the judge of the validity of the contract.

Many people who voted had lost money, so their vote was not based on what they thought was right, but on getting their money back.

To reverse the transactions, the blockchain was reset to the state before the money was stolen.

Most users, including the original creators of Ethereum, had agreed to this.

However, part of the community saw this decision as a kind of violation of the ideology and design of the Ethereum network, and therefore continued to use the Ethereum platform and blockchain without reversing the transaction.

This resulted in two Ethereum blockchains and two currencies in use, which was confusing.

The original blockchain was named Ethereum Classic and the currency Ether Classic.

Ethereum Classic was built on the principles of immutability, neutrality, decentralization, and the idea that the code is the law.

The community believes that the platform should be developed further without interfering with contracts or transactions on the network and without affecting the use of the platform.

Ethereum Classic has all the features of Ethereum, but has a much smaller community and less processing power to support it.

Today, Ethereum Classic is a similar version of Ethereum, but much less supported.

The current price of Ether Classic is about one-tenth of Ether.

The purpose of Ethereum Classic is to differentiate itself, but we can't say for sure that it will have enough support to stand up to Ethereum.

The Ethereum main platform enjoys great support from developers as well as interest from governments and large corporations.

The essential at a glance

- ⇨ Ethereum Classic was ultimately created as a result of a programming error in a smart contract that led to a vote on how to proceed. This resulted in the division of Ethereum and Ethereum Classic.
- ⇨ Ethereum Classic is thus a fork of Ethereum, which is not as significant as Ethereum today.
- ⇨ The market capitalization at the end of 2021 of Ethereum Classic is around USD 5 billion.

Chapter 5:
DApps

Decentralized apps, also known as DApps, are applications that do not have a central server, unlike conventional applications or "apps".

They run over a distributed computer network and do not require a central server or a company to control them in order to function.

DApp users connect directly with each other, and although a company or developer can create a DApp, once it is released it is controlled by the majority of users.

The creator of the DApp cannot censor or centrally control the app.

To better understand how DApps work, we first need to make a distinction between standard apps and DApps, and then between DApps and standard centralized apps.

Centralized applications are installed and run on a central server.

When we access a website, we do so from the same server that everyone else uses.

All data is sent from the central server to all users who access it, but these centralized applications are naturally more vulnerable to hacking.

If the main server is attacked, all user data may be vulnerable and hackers can control the app, and if the main server goes offline, the entire app goes offline as well.

Other features concern

- censorship, as centralized websites, applications and servers can be blocked by governments, and
- the computing power, because the more users are connected to the server, the slower the server will become if the computing power is not constantly increased.

Unlike standard apps, a DApp is not installed on a central server, but on the computers of the various users who contribute their computing power to the app. No higher authority has complete control.

Although we've only been hearing a lot about them recently thanks to blockchain technology, decentralized applications have actually been around since the birth of P2P networks.

One example is BitTorrent, an application that enables file sharing in a distributed manner, i.e., in an online space where various digital assets are stored on computers in different parts of the world.

However, it is only with the blockchain that DApps have seen their growth.

One of their main advantages is their long-term sustainability.

Non-blockchain-based decentralized applications, like BitTorrent for example, need third-party support to improve, fund, and sustain themselves.

This is no longer true for blockchain-based DApps. They are self-sustaining from both an economic and a development perspective.

Moreover, while applications running on the blockchain may have inventors or founders, they will never be the true owners of the decentralized application.

The peculiarity of these unconventional applications lies in the fact that they are open source.

The code they are programmed with is public and can be adopted by others to improve or adapt it to the needs of a specific target.

There are different categories of DApps, but we can divide them into three main categories:

- Type 1 DApps that have their own blockchain and use the original asset of that to be able to function.

- Type 2 DApps that use a Type 1 blockchain protocol.
- Type 3 DApps that use the protocol of Type 2 DApps.

It is important to distinguish between the different types of DApps.

Even though DApps represent an important breakthrough for the applications we already know, it is not necessarily the case that they would be a quantum leap.

In fact, however, many of the features suggest to us that DApps also represent something revolutionary that will solve many of the problems that currently exist among all stakeholders of centralized applications.

There are many technical issues that can make a business idea unfeasible if not addressed.

Possible main problems are:

- Slowness in time-consuming transactions.
- Each time a user wants to use a DApp, a fee is charged.
- DApp is not removable from a network.
- Need to learn new programming languages.
- No usability for the users.

In a DApp, the data is stored in a distributed network. Ownership of the digital resources rests with the users, and the developer has no right of control.

All rules are transparent and cannot be changed without everyone's consent.

In the current app system that has existed so far, the most popular categories that have a large volume are betting and gambling.

A DApp can store documents and certificates, protect a company's strategic data, enable international transactions without intermediaries, enable the exchange of loyalty points or vouchers, etc.

We mentioned BitTorrent in the beginning because it is a simple example to understand how a decentralized system works, but it is not a DApp and it does not run on the Ethereum platform.

DApps on the Ethereum platform work similarly to BitTorrent, but there are key differences.

- DApps are open source, which means that anyone can view the source code and create their own version of the application. Applications like BitTorrent don't have to be open source, and the developers of the application are the only people who can see the source code.
- DApps have an in-app currency or token.

- The Ethereum platform requires developers to pay for computing power in Ether to make applications viable and cover the cost of computing power.
- DApps running on Ethereum can create their own in-app tokens that users can buy and use to pay for additional features in the app.
- For example, sending a message in a messaging app may cost a token. However, the token may only cost a fraction of a cent, so sending a message doesn't cost much.

There are developers who create DApps, but once they are released, changes to the app and decisions about the app are made by the majority of users.

This is a danger of DApps and decentralized networks, as control of the app or network is in the hands of the majority of the network.

Should the majority of users choose this version of the application, it will become the version of the application.

The biggest five DApps[7] running on Ethereum at the time of writing (as measured by number of users over the last 30 days) are:

1. Uniswap
2. Uniswap V3
3. OpenSea
4. MetaMask Swap
5. Sushi

[7] Source: https://dappradar.com/rankings, retrieved 11/16/2021

- ⇨ DApps are decentralized applications.
- ⇨ DApps are distributed, open source and have their own currency/tokens.
- ⇨ Censorship or control of DApps is practically impossible.
- ⇨ Once published, DApps are beyond the control of the creator. Changes must be approved by the community.

6. Chapter: Smart Contracts

Another important innovation that Ethereum has introduced is smart contracts ("smart contracts") that operate on a blockchain.

Smart contracts based on the blockchain have been presented as an absolutely revolutionary concept that could have a major impact on finance, contracts, and almost every industry worldwide in the long run.

But what are smart contracts?

Smart contracts are contracts that can be enforced much like legal contracts, but instead of being written by lawyers and managed by a court, they are written in a programming language and can manage themselves.

As mentioned earlier, traditional contracts are usually drafted by lawyers and include several pages of terms and conditions of an agreement between two parties.

They contain the details of what has been agreed as well as any claims for damages and consequences in the event of non-compliance with the provisions of the contract.

If one of the parties fails to fulfill its part of the contract, the other party can hire an attorney and sue for damages.

Contract terms may be ambiguous, and in any case a contract must be interpreted to some extent.

There have been cases where a simple point has completely changed the meaning of a sentence in a contract.

In contrast, smart contracts are written in source code using the Solidity programming language.

There is no ambiguity in the terms of a source code.

Smart contracts are executed on the Ethereum virtual machine and the Ethereum blockchain, which is connected to the Ethereum cryptocurrency Ether.

As for the terms of the contract, they may refer to payments and indemnities for non-performance of the terms of the contract, all of which are written using the source code.

In the case of a contract for the sale of a business, the smart contract would include ownership of the shares and property rights of the business.

Payment would go to the smart contract rather than directly to the seller, and upon receipt of payment, the smart contract would transfer ownership of the business to the buyer and the sale amount to the seller.

If the buyer does not pay the amount in full or if payment is not received before the due date, the launch agreement would transfer the shares and ownership back to the seller, terminate the agreement, and deny future payments.

One of the main advantages is that smart contracts are written in source code, which prevents misunderstandings about wording and terms. No lawyers or courts are needed to enforce the contract.

If the terms of the contract are met, the contract will be enforced.

If the terms of the contract are not met, the contract is automatically fulfilled and compensation is paid.

Smart contracts are executed on the decentralized Ethereum network, which, as mentioned earlier, reduces the risks of hacking, fraud, server failures, and unauthorized access to contracts.

It is possible to determine the degree of autonomy of the contract. These contracts can be partially or fully self-executing and self-amplifying, and all changes and modifications are recorded in the blockchain.

This creates a permanent record of all changes and actions made to the smart contract.

Smart contracts have a wide network of uses.

Many companies are developing smart contracts that could improve the way existing industries and processes are conducted.

So, in summary, lawyers are being replaced by programmers, anyone can create a smart contract, but few people have the skills to write one.

Developers will have to write them instead of lawyers.

Errors in source code can be much more dangerous than an ambiguous sentence in a contract, because if there were ambiguous sentences in a contract, you could discuss, change, debate, or go to court.

On the other hand, if there is an error in the source code of a contract, the contract will be executed with the erroneous code and cannot be undone or enforced in court.

This was the case with "The DAO", as we have already mentioned in earlier chapters.

You cannot contradict an intelligent contract.

The contract will apply the conditions according to the Code. If a party believes that the contract is unfair or was executed incorrectly due to a mistake or misunderstanding of the terms, there is no way to change the contract. However, there are limits to the types of contracts that can be created.

- It is possible to prove digital ownership of assets; however, this is more complicated for real assets.
- Smart contracts can also make it difficult to determine whether the quality of a contract meets expected standards.
- It is possible to program basic yes/no requests, but it is not possible to determine the quality of this work.
- Software problems can cause errors in smart contracts. Smart contracts run on Ethereum, which relies on a network of computers and programs to function. Problems in the software or network can cause errors in smart contracts.
- Smart contracts are source code that exists outside the legal jurisdiction of any state or country. Should there be a breach of contract or a dispute over the terms of the contract, the smart contract may not have a jurisdiction other than the blockchain. However, the possibility has been presented that a potential arbitration could take place in an arbitration court on the Blockchain that is powered by source code. This is an untested method of creating and enforcing contracts.

Ultimately, legal contracts have been used for many, many years, they may not be perfect, but they have survived many problems.

Smart contracts, on the other hand, are new and have not been tested over an extended period of time, so their use at this very early stage could expose companies to unexpected risks associated with a new technology.

The essential at a glance

- ⇨ Smart contracts are smart contracts that run on the blockchain.
- ⇨ By their very nature, smart contracts are subject to automatism.
- ⇨ The legal handling of smart contracts has not yet been consolidated.

Chapter 7: Advantages and disadvantages

One of the great advantages of Ethereum is the fact that all the individual computers connected in the network act as a kind of giant supercomputer worldwide.

Although the Bitcoin network is also connected like a supercomputer, the computing power of the Bitcoin network is only used to process transactions.

The computing power of the Ethereum network, on the other hand, can be harnessed in the Ethereum Virtual Machine, enabling the creation of applications that thus leverage the power of one of the most powerful supercomputers in the world.

Blockchain technology is quite revolutionary, but before Ethereum, blockchains had limited functionality and were mainly used to record transactions.

One of Ethereum's key innovations compared to existing blockchain technologies is the Ethereum Virtual Machine.

It allows developers to create applications using programming languages similar to what they are used to.

These applications can be as sophisticated as any other applications that can be created on other computing platforms.

They run on the Ethereum Virtual Machine, which allows these decentralized applications to use blockchain technology in a simpler and cheaper way than was possible in the past.

Building a blockchain network is indeed expensive, complex, and time-consuming, as many people need to contribute their computing power to the new blockchain network.

Developers will need to create a new blockchain and build a network of computers and users to support it.

Ethereum allows developers to leverage Ethereum's existing blockchain and computer network.

The Ethereum Virtual Machine also allows developers to build applications on top of blockchain technology without having to build their own blockchain network.

Developing applications that run on the Ethereum blockchain and Ethereum Virtual Machine is quite simple.

The programming language is similar to other widely used languages, such as JavaScript.

Since the programming language is similar to existing languages, developers can easily create programs with little need to learn new concepts.

We may think we have control over our photos on Facebook, the files we store in the cloud, or the messages in our chat program. But in reality, all of these files are controlled by centralized systems and companies.

When we upload photos to Facebook, all images are stored on a central server owned by Facebook.

The same principle applies to files we upload to Google Drive or other cloud storage.

When we send a message through a chat program, the message is sent to the company's central server, which then forwards it from the central server to the recipient.

The server stores all messages.

When we access our chat log, we do so from these servers.

Ethereum allows for decentralization of applications and data, which means there is no central server or company controlling all of our data.

Distributed applications run on a network of computers so that if one computer fails, data can still be accessed from the other computers running the application.

Decentralized versions of many applications and programs that we use every day, such as decentralized cloud storage programs, messaging apps, social networks, etc., are being developed on the Ethereum network.

The decentralized structure of the Ethereum network means that governments and companies cannot censor websites or applications.

If a government wanted to censor a website, it could block access to that website or shut down the server running the website.

If it wanted to censor a decentralized application, it would have to shut down every computer and server running the application. Computers running DApps are all over the world, so it's impossible for a government to shut them all down.

If a user posts an image on Twitter, Facebook or Instagram and the company does not agree, it can remove the image and block the user.

For most people who don't post anything that violates the rules of these sites, this may not be a problem.

However, these companies must comply with the laws of the countries in which they operate.

Most social media platforms are banned in China because foreign companies do not respect the Chinese government's strict censorship.

In China, users who post content deemed critical by the Chinese government will have their posts removed, and may be subject to investigation by the Chinese government for their posts.

Companies operating in China must stop content that is not approved by the government and provide user data to the government.

In contrast, with decentralized networks and applications, governments and corporations cannot censor content, ban applications, or tap user data. This allows for greater freedom of speech and puts control back into the hands of users of applications running on Ethereum.

Many of the risks of existing centralized systems are mitigated by decentralized applications.

Facebook, PayPal, banks and many other companies have centralized servers. If these servers were hacked, hackers could get at all of our personal data stored on these servers. As you have undoubtedly also read on various occasions, exactly such cases have already happened several times.

If the central servers were to crash or go offline, all data would be inaccessible.

Decentralized servers are not as vulnerable to hacker attacks or failures.

To hack a decentralized system, the hacker would need to control most of the network's computing power.

Because the Ethereum network consists of so many computers around the world, it would be impossible for one person to control the entire network. This allows for the high tamper-resistance of smart contracts, which are, after all, written in source code and executed automatically when the contract conditions are met.

Although Bitcoin allows payments to be made on a blockchain, payments are made manually, meaning a decision must be made to send money to another person.

Ethereum, on the other hand, enables automatic payments that can be triggered when an event, threshold, or condition occurs. For example, if you take a cab, the condition could be that you automatically pay the driver at the end of the ride.

Ethereum has created a platform to run decentralized applications (DApps) with smart contracts to replace traditional processes.

Although Initial Coin Offerings existed before Ethereum, they were associated with the popularity of the new cryptocurrency.

Ethereum, on the other hand, allows companies to create their own applications and sell their own tokens or coins, which can then be used in the respective application.

These applications run on the Ethereum platform, and as an application becomes popular, the tokens used in the application should increase in value.

Companies can raise funds for their projects without needing loans or financing. The original backers of the app can also make a profit if the app becomes popular.

However, it also has many disadvantages and thus risks.

By design, Ether is not meant for real transactions.

Ether, the cryptocurrency used for payments on the Ethereum network, is used to pay for the computing power required to execute DApps and smart contracts.

Ether is not in itself intended for payments in stores, online, or as an alternative to other real-world payment methods.

Instead, Bitcoin and many other cryptocurrencies are more practical means of payment that are often accepted in stores and websites around the world.

The use of Ether will depend on the popularity of the Ethereum platform and the number of people running DApps and smart contracts. The value of Ether may not increase, and even if the Ethereum platform becomes more popular, this would not guarantee an increase in the Ether price.

Many of the people buying Ether are buying it to make a speculative profit and do not intend to use it to create DApps or smart contracts.

Today, the Ether price might be overvalued by traders and speculators. If they were to sell, the Ether price could fall quickly.

Even if developers and companies using Ethereum platform need a lot of Ether, the Ether price might not increase if a larger supply of Ether is created or demand from traders decreases.

Ethereum is a new technology. Although it has great potential, as with any new technology, there are still many unknown risks.

Many companies have joined forces to develop the use of Ethereum in their organizations, but are still in the research and feasibility study phase.

There are few companies that have adopted Ethereum as a replacement for existing systems.

There have also been a few mainstream DApps that have become popular. See the list at the end of chapter 5 or directly https://dappradar.com/rankings.

Many of the dangers and risks associated with using Ethereum are unknown today and may not become apparent until Ethereum is widely deployed.

Another risk exists in connection with the use of smart contracts.

The biggest case that shows the problems of smart contracts is the DAO hack, as mentioned earlier.

This type of contract can involve financial risks, but also security risks.

Today, smart contracts are being developed for almost everything, including connections to home appliances, cars, phones, and other electronic systems; almost all armies use computer systems; and some of the most advanced weapons are based on information technology.

Governments are looking for ways to complement blockchain-based technologies and replace existing database systems.

In the event of a bug in the code or poorly written code, there is a possibility that the smart contract would not execute as intended. The contract would then be executed without being able to stop or change it, which would have catastrophic consequences, especially in areas involving government or military systems.

DApps also offer many advantages over existing applications.

However, historically there have been several technologies with advantages over existing options that have not been embraced by the public.

Apps like Instagram or Facebook are free, but they use our personal data so that advertising companies can sell products and services.

They are free to users, but the product these companies sell to others is our personal data.

DApps are controlled by the users, not by a centralized company. Users have control over their privacy and data, and in return, DApps get paid.

Uploading a photo, liking a photo, or other actions on a photo-sharing app could cost a certain amount of money for each action.

It might be difficult to convince people to pay for a new application that is similar to a popular free application.

The privacy and other benefits of decentralization may not be compelling enough to convince people to use DApps instead of existing apps, especially if they have to pay to use them.

The essential at a glance

- ⇨ Ethereum is still a new technology and therefore also associated with many unknowns and risks.
- ⇨ Nevertheless, the system is established.
- ⇨ The essential element is decentralization with all the associated advantages and disadvantages.
- ⇨ Government censorship becomes virtually impossible.

Chapter 8:
The Ethereum Wallet

The components of an Ethereum wallet

An Ethereum wallet consists of a few main components:

1. **Ethereum address** similar to an email address. We give people our Ethereum address so they can send us Ether, just like we give our email address so we can receive email. Our Ethereum address is public. Anyone on the Ethereum network is able to see our account balance and any transactions that have taken place through our address. In addition, an Ethereum wallet can contain multiple addresses.

2. **Private key, which is** the password we use to prove ownership of our Ethereum address in order to access and transfer Ether from that address. So it's important that we don't give our private key to anyone. That would be the same as giving out our ATM pin. Anyone who has our private key has authority over our address and can transfer Ether from our address.

3. **Client / Software, i.e.** in order to access our wallet and perform transactions, we need a software or a way to access our wallet and communicate with the Ethereum network. This is called a client and can be a mobile app, website, or computer program that connects to the network, similar to how we access our bank account and perform transactions through our bank's mobile app or website.

There are different types of wallets for managing and performing transactions on the Ethereum network.

Each of these options has different advantages and disadvantages.

Web Wallet

Let's start with the web wallet, a wallet that can be accessed through a web browser on a computer or mobile device.

The process is similar to logging into your bank's website in the web browser on your computer. Web wallets can be used by both beginners and experts and can be created in a few minutes via a web browser without the need for ID verification.

With web wallets, you do not need to install any applications or software.

All updates to the web wallet are made by the website on its own server, so you do not need to update or download new versions of the web wallet.

It also allow access to our private keys. Usually, there is no customer service or company to contact if you lose your private keys. Just make sure that you secure your private keys yourself and take care of them, otherwise you will lose access to your web wallet. Web wallets are similar to any other website. They can be blocked by governments or providers. Fraudsters can create copies of legitimate web wallet websites with similar names to trick users into logging into the fake website and revealing their private key. Websites can also be hacked, which means that even if it is a legitimate website, a hacked code could be inserted into the website to steal private keys.

It is not possible to buy Ether directly from a web wallet, so you need to create another wallet to buy Ether.

There are services that allow you to buy Ether and transfer it to your web wallet, but they may also require you to verify an identity document. Some web wallets allow you to own Ethereum tokens and participate in ICOs.

Then there are marketplaces, which are similar to stock exchanges or currency markets. They allow traders to buy and sell cryptocurrencies among themselves to profit from price changes.

Within a market, you can have multiple cryptocurrencies in the same account and trade them with each other. They are regulated like financial institutions.

They may also have other features such as customer service and security controls similar to those of traditional online banking sites.

Within a marketplace, private keys are not controlled, although this could pose a risk of private key loss as well as marketplace hacking or bankruptcy.

Today, this risk is lower because the markets are more regulated.

On the markets, you can buy cryptocurrencies using traditional payment methods, but they have long verification procedures.

It is possible to take advantage of the markets and avoid the long verification processes by uploading the cryptocurrencies we already own into our accounts.

Nevertheless, one can speak of a hybrid web wallet/marketplace, which thus combines the features of an Ethereum web wallet with those of a marketplace.

It provides the ability to send and receive Ether like a web wallet and buy or sell Ether at market prices.

Hybrid web wallets/marketplaces allow you to buy Ether using traditional payment methods such as bank accounts and credit cards.

They are usually processed similarly to other financial institutions and require you to prove your identity before you can make purchases.

Since a hybrid web wallet is a combination of a web wallet and a marketplace, it does not have the full functionality of either.

The functions of a hybrid web wallet are not as comprehensive as those of other web wallets, and the functions of the marketplace are not as rich as those of other marketplaces.

With a hybrid web wallet/marketplace, you cannot hold Ethereum tokens or participate in ICOs. Also, you have no control over your private keys, so it is important to use a regulated and trusted company.

For Ethereum newbies, it is also the best option because it offers a user-friendly interface that doesn't require an understanding of the more complicated features of wallets or stock markets.

It also provides an easy way to buy Ether quickly using existing payment methods. So, if you really want to buy Ether only to sell it later for a profit without using any other features, this is the easiest method. Thus, ask your local bank about this or look for another state-supervised bank that also offers cryptocurrency trading.

On the other hand, everyone who owns a smartphone absolutely needs a mobile app.

Mobile Wallets (Apps)

Today, there are apps for all needs, including apps for Ethereum wallets.

These apps offer the ability to buy, sell, and receive Ether and other cryptocurrencies through your smartphone.

Mobile apps are as easy to use and install as any other mobile application.

They have the advantage of allowing you to access your cryptocurrency wallet from your smartphone and are more secure than other options, as they have to meet the security requirements of the app stores.

Since apps must meet certain requirements set by the store, it is not always possible to own Ethereum tokens or buy Ether within the app.

When setting up your mobile app, it is important that you store your backup data, private keys and recovery phrases on another device, not on your phone.

It is a common mistake to store all backup and recovery data on the same device as the wallet. If the device is lost, stolen or broken, both the wallet and the recovery data will be lost.

Although mobile and web applications are becoming more popular than computer software, most people still use multiple programs per day.

Software wallets allow you to install and manage an Ethereum wallet from your computer. They are just a bit more difficult to install and configure, but if you have installed a computer program before, you should have no problems installing them.

Programs downloaded from the Internet can pose more security risks than a mobile app. So be careful and check the website from which you download the program.

Software portfolios have an interface that is displayed on the computer screen and are therefore larger and more user-friendly than a smartphone.

Sometimes they also allow you to have multiple cryptocurrencies and tokens in the same wallet.

It is important to password protect both our computer and our software wallet, and it is also important to store our private keys and recovery phrases on another device or cloud storage service so that they are not on our computer.

A major risk with software wallets is that they do not store passwords and recovery phrases correctly on another device. If our computer is stolen, broken, or infected with a virus, and our only recovery phrases are on the same computer as our wallet, we lose access to the wallet.

Chrome extensions are applications that run inside the Chrome web browser. They can do almost anything a website or software can do and are accessible from the browser's menu bar.

There are Ethereum wallets that are Chrome extensions that allow you to send and receive Ether through your web browser.

One advantage of Chrome extensions is that they can improve the functionality of the websites we visit, for example, by automatically detecting ether addresses on pages or linking to web applications.

However, there are security risks associated with Chrome extensions, as they are easy to create and publish to the Chrome Store.

Not only do they provide advanced functionality for web pages, but they can also read the data we enter into web pages.

Installing Chrome extensions with security issues or malicious extensions could put our personal and financial data at risk, so you need to make sure that you install only trusted extensions.

Although Chrome extensions have the advantage of being in our browser, they can only be accessed from this browser.

They are not like web wallets that can be accessed from any device with an internet connection.

This means that if we lose our computer, it breaks or is stolen, and we don't have a backup copy of our passwords and recovery phrases on another device, we lose access to our wallet.

I am repeating myself here, but please be aware of this risk. There is no place or customer service, like your bank's branch, that you can turn to should your access data be lost or stolen. Also consider the risk of a simple defect in your device!

The paper wallet

Then there is the paper wallet, which is printed on a piece of paper.

This piece of paper contains the public address and QR code of the wallet, which can be issued to other people to send money to this wallet.

When a paper wallet is printed out, the private key may also be on the printout. Therefore, make sure that you remove it and store it in another place.

Paper wallets are not connected to a computer, website, or electronic network, so they are not exposed to the risks of software or web wallets.

They also cannot be hacked and provide a secure way to store Ether.

Since they are not connected to the Ethereum network, you cannot send transactions unless you enter your private key on a website or in software, but this can pose security risks.

Paper wallets can be easily stolen, destroyed or lost. To reduce these risks, they should be laminated.

Private keys can be stored securely in different locations, separate from the wallet's public information.

You cannot really work (buy / sell) with a paper wallet. It is better suited if you have a longer storage of the Ether in mind or just as a backup.

Hardware wallets

Now let's consider hardware wallets. These are electronic devices that store the private keys for an Ethereum or cryptocurrency wallet.

They have similar security features to a paper wallet in that they are not connected to the network except when a transaction is sent, so the Ether remains safe most of the time.

Hardware wallets must be connected to a computer to send transactions, but this poses some security risks.

They are usually designed so that the private key is not revealed when transactions are sent.

Some hardware wallets also allow us to hide wallets with a high balance, in case of theft or in situations where we need to reveal the balance of our hardware wallet.

It is not possible to buy Ether with a hardware wallet, and not all of them allow holding tokens.

It is necessary to have Ether in another way and then transfer it to the hardware wallet.

Hardware wallets are recommended for people who already have some experience with Ethereum and cryptocurrencies.

If you want to keep your Ethers as an asset for a longer period of time, I recommend three possible approaches, combined if necessary.

- Generate a paper wallet and keep it appropriately secured (fireproof!). Make a copy of it as well. Make sure that the colors do not fade. Lamination may be an option. Note, however, that even in a fire safe, great heat can be generated and the lamination may melt.

- Use a hardware wallet. To enable future-proof use (even in e.g. 10 years), I would still record the key separately (paper or storage, see after).

- Save your key in a secure (!) cloud. I would only do this in specially secured clouds, i.e. not the usual ones like offered by the big internet companies. There again, make sure that your access data to the cloud is secure.

A combination of the three methods seems to me to be the safest.

It is best to put your access data, paper key or hardware wallet in your bank safe.

The essential at a glance

- ⇨ There are several ways you can hold Ether. You need to find the most suitable one for you.
- ⇨ If you want to work with Ether efficiently, you need a mobile or a software wallet.
- ⇨ Paper or hardware wallets are recommended for security.
- ⇨ Place the backups in your bank drawer.

Chapter 9: Uses

Once you open a wallet, you will be able to use the Ethereum network and thus all related operations.

The easiest way to get started with Ether is to buy it using traditional payment methods such as bank transfers or credit cards.

There are several ways you can buy Ether.

Create an account e.g. on Coinbase or Binance or open an account on a marketplace (e.g. Kraken) or buy Ether with a credit card.

In order to receive Ether in our wallet, we need to give the person or service that will send us Ether our address. It's a bit like giving someone your IBAN so they can wire us.

There are two ways to specify this address: either by specifying the public key, which is a unique sequence of letters and numbers, or by specifying the QR code.

Another operation is sending ether, which is similar to receiving ether.

In this case, we need the Ethereum address or QR code to send Ether.

In our Ethereum wallet, we can select "Send" by pressing the corresponding button.

Then we are asked for the amount in Ether and the address to send it to.

The Ether amount can be expressed in dollars, but is usually expressed in units such as one Ether, 0.5 Ether, and so on.

We can copy and paste the address where the ether should be sent or scan the QR code.

In this context, it is **immensely important to** carefully check if the address is correct, because if we send Ether to a wrong address, there is no way to cancel the transaction and we will lose our Ether.

Once we have verified that the amount and address are correct, we can send the Ether to the recipient.

Once we have bought or received Ether, we may want to exchange it for other cryptocurrencies.

So we could do with trading Ether through a market the same way we would trade stocks or currencies.

We can use our Ether to buy other cryptocurrencies held in a portfolio for each cryptocurrency on the market.

This can be an easy way to receive and hold a number of different cryptocurrencies in one account.

Trading cryptocurrencies to profit from price fluctuations is considered speculative and carries a high level of risk.

It is also possible to trade Ether in exchange for computing power to run decentralized applications and smart contracts on the Ethereum network.

Generally, trading Ether requires access to an exchange with a virtual wallet.

Trading Ether can guarantee high profits, but it also has its risks.

For those who want to invest in Ethereum, that is, trade with the aim of making as much profit as possible, Contracts for Difference (CFDs) are the best instrument.

Investing in Ethereum by trading CFDs is quite easy, safe and essentially, you can make money with it both when the value of Ethereum increases and when it decreases.

When you trade this way, you can either go up, i.e. buy, or go down, i.e. sell short.

If your prediction is correct, you profit.

Profits are proportional to the price difference, but can be multiplied thanks to a leverage effect.

So, to sum up, trading Ethereum can be a high-yield activity considering that it is a cryptocurrency with high volatility.

For maximum profits, we recommend trading with a safe, reliable platform that allows you to buy and sell Ethereum short.

This way you can trade profitably and make money on both rising and falling Ethereum prices.

The essential at a glance

- ⇨ You can now trade Ether through many banks that offer cryptocurrency transactions.
- ⇨ If you want to trade yourself, a software mobile wallet is recommended. Use it to log in to Coinbase or Binance, for example.
- ⇨ For intensive trading you better work with CFDs.

Chapter 10: The Future of Ethereum

The future of Ethereum is still very uncertain.

It is not yet known whether governments and large enterprises will replace existing systems with Ethereum-based solutions.

It is still a very new cryptocurrency and the applications based on it are very simple.

In the early days of the Internet, most websites were just text and a few links. It took many years before websites were as developed as we know them today.

Ethereum's current capabilities may pale in comparison to its future possibilities. Today's DApps are comparable to the text-only websites that existed in the early days of the Internet.

At the moment, we can only guess what the future of Ethereum will bring. Considering the speed at which the technology is advancing, it could exceed our expectations.

However, it is possible that after analyzing Ethereum, companies and governments decide not to use it anyway.

They may decide to develop their own blockchain-based systems that are not based on the Ethereum platform.

However, given the number of governments and companies interested in Ethereum, it is already safe to assume that Ethereum will be used by large companies and governments.

Even if companies in the alliance do not choose Ethereum, there are thousands of other companies not in the alliance hoping to use Ethereum for their businesses.

Whether smart contracts, DApps, and the Ethereum platform become more popular certainly depends on positive public acceptance.

Most people are not interested in terms like "decentralization" or "censorship-proof," but much more in terms like "security."

For most people, there is no need to use DApps and smart contracts, and the benefits may not be attractive compared to existing options.

For many people, the elimination of third-party intermediaries is not beneficial because they cannot contact customer service or visit a physical location.

If companies can create DApps that are attractive to a mass market, then people will use Ethereum to be able to use those DApps.

If there are no DApps that users want to use, or no compelling reasons to use them, then they are unlikely to become popular or replace current options.

Ethereum continues to be a major revolution in the cryptocurrency space.

At the time of writing, there are also uncertainties about how large states will deal with cryptocurrencies in general. Regulatory questions about financial intermediaries trading cryptocurrencies are looming. Certain states are reacting restrictively (China, Algeria, Morocco and others), while other states are using cryptocurrencies officially (Switzerland, El Salvador, USA and others). For a current overview, see: https://en.wikipedia.org/wiki/Legality_of_bitcoin_by_country_or_territory

The essential at a glance

- ⇨ Ethereum's future is still uncertain.
- ⇨ However, the uncertainty hangs on cryptocurrencies in general. Ethereum itself is very well positioned.
- ⇨ A general trend of how states deal with cryptocurrencies is not yet foreseeable.
- ⇨ Blockchain technology is here to stay no matter what.
- ⇨ With Ethereum 2.0 and the shift to less energy-intensive proof-of-stake, Ethereum will take an important step towards a (more) sustainable future in 2022.

About Thomas J. Taylor

Thomas J. Taylor is professionally involved with cryptocurrencies, banking and other financial services. He has published several books on Bitcoin, Ethereum, cryptocurrencies, technical analysis and other financial topics.

www.ingramcontent.com/pod-product-compliance
Lightning Source LLC
LaVergne TN
LVHW090422210926
848480LV00002B/653